May this book bring blessing to all those who read it.

There is so much He wants to tell us.
He wants us to spend time to be with Him.

© 2018-2023 Chelsea Kong

All rights reserved. All images used in this book are licensed copies from their respectful owners. This book or any portion thereof may not be reproduced or used in any manner whatsoever without the express written permission of the publisher except for the use of brief quotations in a book review.

Printed in 2019-2023, Made in Toronto, Canada
Hard Copy ISBN: 978-1-990399-73-2
Library and Archives Canada

HOW TO HEAR GOD'S VOICE

Know His Voice

By Chelsea Kong

Read His Word and remember it.
Meditate on the Word.
Write it out.
Speak God's Word.

Find a place to be alone with God.
Find in a quiet place and let God speak to you.

Use a book to write, draw, or record God's words. Use a pen, pencil, crayons, pastels, or markers.

We need to be quiet to hear God speak.
He wants our full attention.
Keep your mind, heart, and soul quiet.

You need God's faith to hear Him.
He will talk, show, or give you an idea.
Faith lets us receive from God.

See God with you.

Imagine Jesus talking to you.

Picture Holy Spirit teaching you.

Know who speaks and let God speak to you.

God is our Father and
He loves to tell us things.

Jesus also wants to share with us.

Holy Spirit will tell us about Jesus.

God also speaks to us through:

Family and Relatives
Angels
Church Leaders and God's People
Friends, Work, and Strangers

God gives us pictures.

Visions

Dreams

People, places, things, and invisible things.

A quiet small voice and a voice like your daddy.

He gives us thoughts and lets us know things.

Words, the Bible, and the future for you or others.

Ideas

Feelings with your body and other feelings

Remember what He gives you and do it.

Keep it your heart, see it, speak it, and hear it.

Do it every day.

Keep it with you when you go out.

Think about it.

Keep praying until something happens.

God promised His angels to watch over us.

Obey God, Jesus, and
Holy Spirit what they say.

God tells us also to obey His Word (Bible)
and His leaders.

Obey your parents.

Obey His teaching and God's word about your future.

Share what God, Jesus, and Holy Spirit tell you to share.

See if it matches the way He talks in the Bible.

Your family and friends
need to know what He says.

God may give you a word
for others about their future.

God may give you a word through others.

Practice listening every day, so God can talk to you.

You hear Him better and then you will know His voice.

You can tell others what God wants you to tell them.

God, I know that I have sinned against you. Forgive me for the wrong that I have done. I believe that Jesus Christ died on the cross for me and that He rose from the grave after three days, so that I can have His long-lasting life. Come into my heart to be my Lord and Savior. I choose to turn away from the wrong I did and choose to follow you. Lead me to walk with you. Keep me safe and teach me your ways. Stop every bad thing in my life that has an open door to hurt me. Close those doors. Holy Spirit, fill me now in Jesus' name. Amen.

Baptism in the Holy Spirit

Jesus, you are the one that fills me with Your Spirit. Come Holy Spirit and come into my life and fill me to overflow with Your presence. Come with your fire too. Thank you for the gift of tongues in Jesus' name. Amen.

Open your mouth and let the words come out that God gives you. It will be words that you don't know what they mean. God can give you the meaning when you ask Him. Keep giving God your mouth to speak it out. You need to let Him talk through you every day to grow this gift. He will also take you closer to God and you will know more about Jesus and have power from God to do great things and know things.

Prayer

Father God, open my ears to hear You. Help me be quiet and to wait for You to talk to me. Open my eyes. Show me what you want me to know. Thank you for your words, pictures, dreams, visions, and voice. Help me do what you want me to do in Jesus' name. Make us smart, so I can help others in Jesus' name. Amen.

Message from the Author

The Lord put it on my heart to write this book to teach children how to hear His voice, but the priority is to know His word before we can hear Him. Most Christians do not know how to hear the voice of God or know that God speaks to them. In our world, it is so important for us to know His voice and His Word. It protects us from evil and danger that we do not expect. Many people have been saved because they heard God speak to them and they quickly followed His instruction. He can tell us about the past, present, and future. He just wants us to listen to Him and do what He says.

Other Products

The Bridal Collection	Counting the Omer
Knowing God	Festival of Lights
How to Hear God's Voice	Glory, Presence, and Holy Spirit
New Life in Jesus	Live in God's Presence
Loving Israel	31 Day Devotional
God's Gifts	Biblical Puzzle Book Vol 1
Meeting God	Biblical Puzzle Book Vol 2
Word Power	Bibllical Puzzle Book Vol 3
Fruit of the Spirit	Biblical Puzzle Book Vol 4
The Tabernacle	Biblical Puzzle Book Vol 5
Bride for Jesus	Bible Puzzles for Young Children Book 1
A Life of Prayer	
Live Free	Bible Puzzles for Young Children Book 2
Who am I in Jesus	
Walk in Love	Bible Puzzles for Young Children Book 3
God's Favor	
Man of God	Biblical Puzzles for Children Book 1
Woman of God	Biblical Puzzles for Children Book 2
How to Use Money	Biblical Puzzles for Children Book 3
God's Wisdom	
Fasting	Teaching Series & Guides
See Jerusalem and Bethany	How to Hear God's Voice Teaching Guide
First Fruit Offering	Knowing God, Jesus, and Holy Spirit
Pentecost	Relationship with God, Jesus, Holy Spirit Guide
Feast of Trumpets	
Day of Atonement	
Feast of Tabernacles	And many more!

Please check Chelsea's website for links to other books and products found on Amazon, Barnes and Noble, and Kobo. Please leave a review to help the author to write more books. Thank you!

https://chelseak532002550.wordpress.com

Coaching Products

Teaching Series Packages to train you
and to equip you for God's purpose!

Check the website for details:
https://chelseak532002550.wordpress.com

Learn How to Hear God's Voice
Knowing Him
Build a Relationship with Him

Each package includes lessons and
related books and audiobooks.

Books can be purchased
separatedly through Amazon.

Coaching Products

Teaching Series Packages to train you and to equip you for God's purpose!

Check the website for details:
https://chelseak532002550.wordpress.com

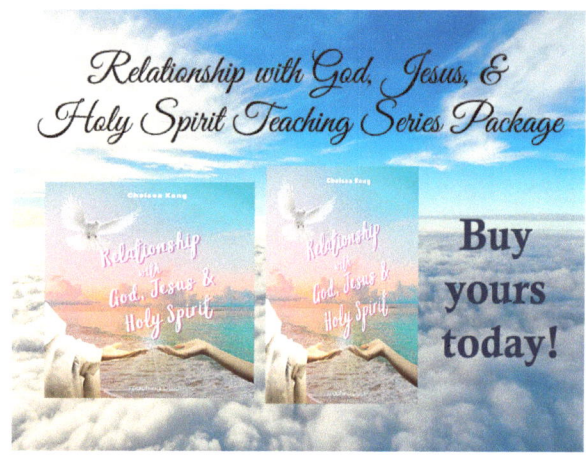

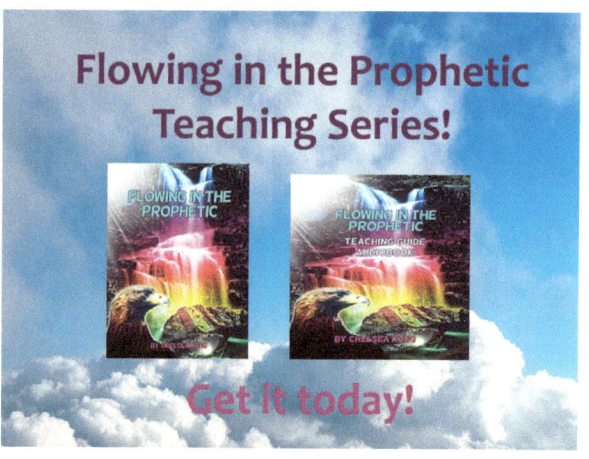

Learn how to build a Relationship with Him and Flow in the Prophetic

Each package includes lessons and related books and audiobooks.

Books can be purchased separatedly through Amazon.

Review

Please leave a review where you purchased the book so that I can share with others and encourages me to continue to write more books. Please share my books with your others.

My books can be found on Amazon, Barnes and Noble, Kobo, and Smashwords. Retailers can also purchase my hard copy books through IngramSpark.

Thank you for reading!

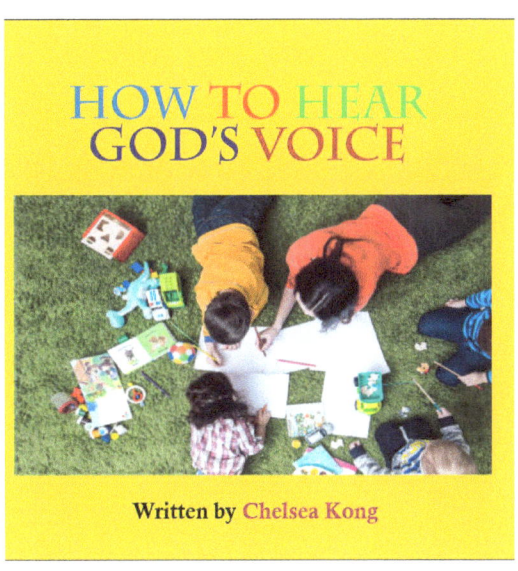

Chelsea Kong Biography

She is a writer, creative arts and digital media artist, and skilled administrative professional. Graduated from Hotel and Restaurant Management, Digital Media Arts, and Office Administration, She also served in a variety of roles from audiovisual, photography, to assisting on the worship team, and ministry team. She has a passion for families being united. Her writing consists of children's books, stories, bridal writing, poems, lyrics for songs, words of encouragement, blessings, prayers, and jokes. She also has her own podcast channel is called Chelsea K on Anchorfm, Spotify, iTunes, etc and podcasts on YouTube. Chelsea has been on Unity Live Radio and The Lady Tracey Show, and published an article on Woman of God in ReadersMagnet in the Author Lounge.

www.ingramcontent.com/pod-product-compliance
Lightning Source LLC
Chambersburg PA
CBHW041414010526
44107CB00016B/1163